CITIZENSHIP IN THE NATION

D0067675

"Enhancing our youths' competitive edge through merit badges"

BOY SCOUTS OF AMERICA®

Requirements

1. Explain what citizenship in the nation means and what it takes to be a good citizen of this country. Discuss the rights, duties, and obligations of a responsible and active American citizen.

2. Do TWO of the following:

   a. Visit a place that is listed as a National Historic Landmark or that is on the National Register of Historic Places. Tell your counselor what you learned about the landmark or site and what you found interesting about it.

   b. Tour your state capitol building or the U.S. Capitol. Tell your counselor what you learned about the capitol, its function, and its history.

   c. Tour a federal facility. Explain to your counselor what you saw there and what you learned about its function in the local community and how it serves this nation.

   d. Choose a national monument that interests you. Using books, brochures, the internet (with your parent's permission), and other resources, find out more about the monument. Tell your counselor what you learned, and explain why the monument is important to this country's citizens.

3. Watch the national evening news five days in a row OR read the front page of a major daily newspaper five days in a row. Discuss the national issues you learned about with your counselor. Choose one of the issues and explain how it affects you and your family.

35871
ISBN 978-0-8395-3248-4
©2014 Boy Scouts of America
2016 Printing

4. Discuss each of the following documents with your counselor. Tell how you feel life in the United States might be different without each one. Then choose one document and explain how it impacts you and your family.

   a. Declaration of Independence

   b. Preamble to the Constitution

   c. The Constitution

   d. Bill of Rights

   e. Amendments to the Constitution

5. List the six functions of government as noted in the preamble to the Constitution. Discuss with your counselor how these functions affect your family and local community.

6. With your counselor's approval, choose a speech of national historical importance. Find out about the author, and tell your counselor about the person who gave the speech. Explain the importance of the speech at the time it was given, and tell how it applies to American citizens today. Choose a sentence or two from the speech that has significant meaning to you, and tell your counselor why.

7. Name the three branches of our federal government and explain to your counselor their functions. Explain how citizens can be involved in each branch. Explain the importance of our checks and balances system. Describe how each branch "checks" and "balances" the others.

8. Name your two senators and a member of Congress from your congressional district. Write a letter about a national issue and send it to one of these elected officials, sharing your view with him or her. Show your letter to your counselor, along with any response you might receive.

Contents

What the Fighting Was All About 7

The Foundation of American Democracy 11

Branches of Government 25

Parties, Splinters, and Special Interests 33

National Issues 39

National Treasures and Other Government Structures 43

Resources 46

What the Fighting Was All About

America certainly has changed since immigrants first settled here. Yet the government the colonists established in the late 1700s has remained intact because people believed in the basic concepts of American democracy:

- The fundamental value and dignity of every individual
- The right to equality before the law, without regard to the individual's social status
- The belief in majority rule and minority rights
- The need for compromise
- The understanding that there are limitations to the federal government's powers; the states and the people have more authority

As long as citizens continue to value these concepts, our government will exist. But if citizens become complacent and take their rights and freedoms for granted, then our rights will be endangered.

". . . I know not what course others may take; but as for me, give me liberty or give me death!"
—From American statesman and orator Patrick Henry's call to arms speech, March 23, 1775

Under other forms of government, people are told how to live and what to believe. In our representative republic, U.S. citizens enjoy freedom and govern themselves through elected representatives. But to experience the full expression of individual freedom, each citizen must govern himself so that his own behavior doesn't interfere with the freedoms of others.

A *democracy* is a form of government in which the people have the power to govern themselves. The citizens exercise their power directly or indirectly through representatives chosen in free elections. The majority rules.

The Founding Fathers established a *republic*— with an elected president (instead of a monarch) as head of state and freely elected representatives who are responsible to the citizens and govern according to law. The Democratic and Republican political parties borrow their names from these forms of government, and both parties support democracy and the republican form of representative government.

Active citizens are aware of and grateful for their liberties and rights. They participate in their governments by voting in elections, attending public hearings, serving on juries, and paying taxes. They protect freedom, help defend our country, and stand up for individual rights on behalf of all U.S. citizens. Like the people who fought for our independence, good citizens today are patriots.

As you fulfill the requirements for this merit badge, think about what *you* can do for your country.

"And so, my fellow Americans:
Ask not what your country can do
for you—ask what you can do for
your country."
—From President John F. Kennedy's
inaugural address, January 20, 1961

The Foundation of American Democracy

Most free colonists brought with them to America the expectation that they would have at least as many rights as they had in the old country. For centuries in England, British subjects—first the privileged classes and then all people—had been protected from the arbitrary (random) acts of the monarch.

A *monarchy* is a form of government in which a hereditary ruler governs for life. In the past, the monarch claimed absolute authority. Today, a monarch reigns but often does not rule.

In 1215, English barons, tired of the Crown's heavy-handed tactics, forced King John to sign the Magna Carta to establish that the power of the monarchy was not absolute. It set forth certain basic rights such as trial by jury and due process of law (acted out fairly and according to established rules), and protected people from the monarch taking any life, liberty, or property at will.

In the 1600s, the English Parliament—a representative legislative body—insisted that the reigning monarchs sign the Petition of Right and the English Bill of Rights. These documents prevented further abuses by limiting the powers of the king and queen. For example, they could no longer:

- Imprison or punish any person except by the legal judgment of his peers, or by law.

- Impose martial law, or have a standing army during peacetime without the consent of Parliament.

- Demand that homeowners allow the king's troops in their home without the owners' permission.

- Make individuals pay a tax without the common consent of Parliament.
- Suspend or execute laws without the consent of Parliament.
- Prosecute anyone for petitioning or making a formal written request to the king.

Although the new American colonists owed allegiance to the British monarch, they believed that a government across the Atlantic Ocean should not meddle in their local affairs. Property owners voted directly in town hall meetings; they elected representatives to their assemblies or gatherings to pass laws and levy taxes. No wonder they bristled when King George III tried to tighten his control over the 13 colonies. He imposed new taxes, restricted trade, and insisted that British troops stationed in the colonies should be allowed to stay in private homes.

Networking Before E-mail

Fearing that the British government had a plan to abolish guaranteed liberties, Samuel Adams organized the Boston Committee of Correspondence to link all the towns in Massachusetts. Post riders (mail carriers on horseback) delivered intelligence reports about British acts affecting the colonies. Soon this intercolonial information network helped unify many colonists in opposition to British policies.

The colonists resisted the British by refusing to purchase English products, by refusing to pay certain taxes, and by throwing tea overboard in Boston Harbor. In response, King George III further restricted the colonists' rights, enacting what were called the "Intolerable Acts." The colonists had to make a choice: Submit to the king's authority as British subjects—or revolt. Colonists organized into the First Continental Congress, a convention of delegates to resist the "Intolerable Acts."

Declaration of Independence

Representatives from the 13 colonies formed the Second Continental Congress and asked statesmen Thomas Jefferson, John Adams, Benjamin Franklin, Robert R. Livingston, and Roger Sherman to write a statement of independence. Led by Jefferson, the committee drew on popular political and social theories, particularly the ideas of English philosopher John Locke and French philosopher Jean Jacques Rousseau. In *The Social Contract,* Rousseau stated that people are basically good, and that government should be run according to the will of the majority. Locke's *Two Treatises of Government* explained that people are born with natural rights (life, liberty, property) and they form "states" or governments to protect those rights.

In Jefferson's draft, the declaration asserted the right of the people to "dissolve the political bands that have connected them with another" and choose their own government. After much argument and compromise, the Second Continental Congress adopted the final version of the Declaration of Independence on July 4, 1776.

Thomas Jefferson was only 33 years old when he drafted the Declaration of Independence.

The Declaration of Independence has five main parts:

1. The preamble, which explains why the declaration was written
2. A series of "self-evident" truths about the rights of all men and the principles of government to which the people were committed
3. A list of 27 specific complaints against King George III
4. A summary of the efforts the colonists made to avoid a break with England
5. A declaration that the 13 colonies are "free and independent" states, completely separate from Great Britain

The Declaration of Independence is the United States of America's birth certificate. But the truths described refer to "all men," not just Americans. This document had a profound impact on the French Revolution and revolts in South America, where countries fought to win their independence from Spain. Today, the declaration continues to inspire the fight for freedom around the world.

Constitution

People depend on government to assure freedom and order, but recognize it as a possible source of harm and oppression. The Founding Fathers wanted to establish a strong central authority but limit its ability to abuse power. Their first attempt at forming a government was a confederation of states. The Articles of Confederation granted independence to each state and gave little authority to the central government.

Under this confederation, each state minted its own money and regulated its own trade. This caused confusion and an economic slump in the United States. In 1786, thousands of farmers in western Massachusetts, led by Daniel Shays, attempted to prevent the courts from foreclosing mortgages on their farms. The central government could not deal with the uprising and the country's economic problems, so the states called for a convention to review the Articles of Confederation.

Delegates at the convention recognized the weaknesses in the document:

- Each state had only one vote, regardless of its size and population.
- Congress had no power to collect taxes and duties.
- Congress had no power to regulate interstate and foreign commerce.
- There were no provisions for a national court system.
- An amendment could be ratified (approved) only with the consent of *all* states.
- A $9/13$ majority was required to enact a law.
- The Articles were at best "a firm league of friendship" among the states.

A majority of the representatives at the convention decided that the problems of the republic could be addressed only by forming a new government and writing a new constitution. The Federalists, led by James Madison and Alexander Hamilton, favored a strong central government and supported ratification of a constitution.

The Anti-Federalists, led by Patrick Henry and John Hancock, objected to ratification mainly because they feared the central government would become too powerful, and the constitution did not include a bill of rights.

After much compromise and debate, a U.S. Constitution was ratified based on the following principles.

Popular sovereignty. The people have supreme power. They establish the government, which is subject to the will of the people.

Limited government. The government may do only what the people have empowered it to do.

Separation of powers. The responsibilities of the government are divided among the executive, legislative, and judicial branches.

Checks and balances. Each branch of government has the authority and responsibility to check (restrain) the power of the other two branches. This balance prevents the misuse of power by any one branch.

Judicial review. Since 1803 it has been established that the federal courts have the power to review acts of the executive and legislative branches. If the court decides that an act or law violates a provision of the Constitution, it can nullify (cancel) the act.

Federalism. Power is shared between national and local governments. This system ensures that the national government is powerful enough to be effective, but that some powers (or functions) are reserved to the states and the citizens themselves.

Preamble to the Constitution

The preamble is the introduction to the Constitution. Only one sentence long, the preamble states the six reasons for creating the document that embodies the basic principles and laws of the United States.

The preamble clearly affirms that the *people*—not the states, not the central government—have the sovereign (supreme and absolute) authority to ordain (establish) the Constitution as the supreme law of the land. The people's intention is to:

"We the People of the United States, in Order to form a more perfect Union, establish Justice, insure domestic Tranquility, provide for the common defense, promote the general Welfare, and secure the Blessings of Liberty to ourselves and our Posterity, do ordain and establish this Constitution for the United States of America."

- Strengthen the country by unifying the states.

- Enact and apply laws that treat all citizens reasonably, fairly, and impartially.

- Maintain order to ensure peace on home soil.

- Make sure that the country is prepared to defend itself from its enemies.

- Provide services and make efforts to improve the quality of life for all citizens.

- Preserve and protect the rights and liberties of Americans, and to pass those freedoms on to future generations.

Articles

In his 1863 Gettysburg Address, President Abraham Lincoln defined American democracy as *"government of the people, by the people, for the people."*

The seven Articles of the Constitution lay the foundation for the United States' system of government. They establish three separate and distinct branches of government; define the relationships of the states between themselves and with the federal government; describe the procedures for amendment; state that the Constitution is the "supreme law of the land"; and explain how the Constitution will be ratified.

Article I establishes the Congress—the legislative, or lawmaking, branch of government that consists of the Senate and the House of Representatives. This article explains the powers and limits of the legislature, the qualifications for office, and the methods of electing representatives. It also places some restrictions on state governments.

Article II establishes the executive branch of government and the offices of the president and vice president. This article explains the powers, duties, and limits of the president and the qualifications and methods of electing the president and vice president.

Electoral College

Have you ever seen a college sweatshirt with the name "Electoral College" on it? Probably not. That's because it's not an actual college, but instead is the name of the group of people who elect the president. The number of these electors in each state is determined by and equal to its number of senators and members of Congress. Each political party appoints that number of electors to cast all their votes for the party's candidate. It's a winner-takes-all system—that means that when a candidate wins a state by even the slightest margin, that person gets all the electoral votes for that state.

The Founding Fathers' original intent for the Electoral College was to allow each state a delegation of informed and knowledgeable people who would select the president based on merit and without regard to political party. Many people believe the Electoral College is a flawed system because it does not exactly reflect the popular vote. In seventeen presidential elections, presidents who did not receive a majority of the popular vote got elected because they were able to get a majority of the electoral votes.

Article III establishes the judicial branch of government and the Supreme Court. This article also gives Congress the power to establish other "inferior" courts. The article explains the judicial power of federal courts.

Article IV, adopted almost exactly from the Articles of Confederation, describes the relationships the states must have with one another, the relationships between the federal government and the state governments, and the procedure for adding states and territories.

Article V details the procedures for amending, or making formal changes to, the Constitution.

Article VI states that the Constitution and all subsequent federal laws are the supreme law of the land. This article requires all state judges to follow the Constitution, even if state laws or constitutions contradict it, and requires all legislative, judicial, and executive officials of the federal and state governments to swear under oath to support the Constitution.

Article VII explains how the Constitution shall be ratified, or approved, by the states in order for it to be established.

According to Article VII, only nine states had to approve the Constitution for it to go into effect in those states. On June 21, 1788, New Hampshire—the ninth state—ratified the Constitution and made it officially the law of the land. But several states refused to ratify the document until Congress agreed to add a list of basic rights held by the people. This list became the Bill of Rights.

Bill of Rights

The first 10 amendments to the Constitution are called the Bill of Rights. These amendments, which guarantee individual rights and freedoms, were added to the Constitution less than three years after it became effective. James Madison drafted the Bill of Rights, borrowing key points from the Magna Carta. These amendments do not give us new liberties; they protect the liberties we already have.

The **First Amendment** is perhaps the most well-known. It protects freedom of religion, speech, and the press, and grants citizens the rights to peaceably assemble and to petition the government.

Agree to Disagree

Supreme Court Justice Oliver Wendell Holmes Jr. (1902–32) urged people to think of free speech as "the principle of free thought—not free thought for those who agree with us but freedom for thought that we hate."

The **Second Amendment** is one of the most controversial of the 10 amendments. It asserts every state's right to have a "well-regulated militia" and the right of the people to have and carry weapons.

The **Third Amendment** protects citizens from being forced to take soldiers into their homes to feed and board them. The exception to this is in wartime if Congress enacts a law requiring that citizens do so.

The **Fourth Amendment** prohibits the unreasonable search and seizure of people, their houses, papers, and private property. In most cases, searches, seizures, and arrests require a warrant issued by a judge.

The **Fifth Amendment** describes the rights of citizens in criminal cases. A person may not stand trial for a serious crime punishable by death or imprisonment unless a grand jury decides there is enough evidence against the individual to bring that person to trial. A citizen may not be tried twice for the same offense (this is called *double jeopardy*), and may not be forced to testify against himself or herself. This amendment also states that no person shall be deprived of life, liberty, or property without "due process of law," or fair and legal procedures. The last provision deals with "eminent domain," or the government's power to take private property for public use. It prevents the government from taking the property without paying the owner a fair price.

> Unlike the First Amendment, which protects your right to speak out, the Fifth Amendment protects your right to keep quiet and not reveal incriminating facts against yourself.

The **Sixth Amendment** guarantees the right to a fair trial. A person charged with a crime must have a speedy and public trial heard by an impartial jury. The defendant has the right to be told of the charges against him or her, be confronted by the accuser, be allowed to introduce witnesses for him or herself, and have the benefit of legal counsel.

The **Seventh Amendment** guarantees the right to a trial by jury in civil cases where the disputed amount exceeds $20. Either party in the suit may ask for a jury trial.

The **Eighth Amendment** prohibits courts from imposing excessive bails and fines. It also forbids the use of "cruel and unusual punishment."

Does the Punishment Fit the Crime?

Americans debate every day about whether the death penalty is a cruel and unusual punishment for a person convicted of murder. Some people argue that paddling students for breaking school rules is cruel and unusual. What do you think?

The **Ninth Amendment** makes clear that the rights mentioned in the first eight amendments include certain, but not *all*, rights of the citizens. It states that the people retain any rights not specifically listed in the Constitution.

The **10th Amendment** asserts that the states or the people retain those powers not delegated to the federal government by the Constitution.

In all of world history, the Bill of Rights is one of the greatest documents protecting individual rights. It has provoked protest rallies, legal challenges, even riots, as Americans interpret and defend their rights. Some of the most hotly debated subjects include gun control, abortion rights, school prayer, censorship, and the teaching of the theory of evolution. No matter where you stand on these issues, the First Amendment guarantees that you can voice your opinion.

Changing the Constitution

Written words in the Constitution can be changed or added through the *formal* amendment process described in Article V. An amendment may be proposed in one of two ways: by a two-thirds vote in each house of Congress; or by a national convention called by Congress at the request of two-thirds of the state legislatures. The proposed amendment may be ratified in one of two ways: by three-fourths of the state legislatures; or by three-fourths of the states during conventions called for that purpose.

In the *informal* amendment process, changes in the Constitution take place over time without altering or adding to the written words. These informal amendments develop as a result of congressional legislation, presidential actions, Supreme Court decisions, activities of political parties, and custom.

Amendments to the Constitution

The Constitution is a flexible document that adapts to the changing needs of American society. Since the Bill of Rights was adopted, the Constitution has been amended 17 times.

The **11th Amendment** (1795) prohibits a citizen of one state or a citizen of another country from suing another state in federal court. However, a citizen may file suit in federal court against state authorities for depriving that person of constitutional rights.

The **12th Amendment** (1804) requires members of the Electoral College to cast two separate ballots: one for president and one for vice president.

It's a Tie

When the Founding Fathers wrote Article II of the Constitution, they planned one election for both president and vice president. Electors each had two votes to cast for two people without specifying the office. The person with the most votes became president and the runner-up became vice president. In the election of 1800, however, Thomas Jefferson tied Aaron Burr. The House of Representatives, after much argument, decided the outcome of the election by casting more ballots for Jefferson.

The **13th Amendment** (1865) abolished slavery in the United States and in territories under its jurisdiction.

The **14th Amendment** (1868) declares that "all persons born or naturalized in the United States" and under its authority are citizens of the United States and in the state in which they live. The intention of this amendment, known as the *civil rights amendment,* was to give citizenship to former slaves. The amendment also forbids states to pass and enforce laws depriving people of their privileges as citizens. It prohibits states from denying people equal protection of their laws or from depriving a person of life, liberty, or property without "due process of law."

The **15th Amendment** (1870) prohibits the U.S. government and the states from denying any citizen the right to vote on account of race, color, or having been a slave. The amendment also asserts that states must extend to the citizens within their jurisdiction all the protections guaranteed in the Bill of Rights.

The **16th Amendment** (1913) grants Congress the right to levy an income tax without regard to each state's population.

The **17th Amendment** (1913) gives the people of the states the power to elect their senators. This amendment repealed those parts of Article I relating to the election of U.S. senators by state legislatures.

The **18th Amendment** (1919), known as the *prohibition amendment,* prohibits the manufacture, sale, and transportation of alcoholic beverages in the United States.

The **19th Amendment** (1920), also known as the *Susan B. Anthony amendment,* prohibits the U.S. government and the states from denying any woman the right to vote.

"It was we, the people; not we, the white male citizens; nor yet we, the male citizens; but we, the whole people, who formed this Union."

—From Susan B. Anthony's speech defending a woman's right to vote, 1873

The **20th Amendment** (1933), often called the *lame duck amendment*, changes the dates that newly elected presidents and members of Congress take office, moving the inaugurations closer to the date of the elections (January 20 for the president, January 3 for Congress).

Lame Ducks

When the Constitution was written in 1787, travel from one part of the country to another was slow and difficult. For this reason, Article I and the 12th Amendment allowed plenty of time for newly elected officials to make their way from their home states to the nation's capital. However, those representatives who were defeated or chose not to run for another term had to serve four to 13 more months before their successors were inaugurated. These officials were called *lame ducks* because they worked without power or prestige. But by 1933, with trains and cars available, elected representatives could arrive at the capital in a shorter period of time.

The **21st Amendment** (1933) repealed the 18th Amendment (prohibition amendment) in its entirety.

The **22nd Amendment** (1951) limits a president's term of office to two terms. It also limits the term of office of a president who has served more than two years of another's term to one elected term.

The **23rd Amendment** (1961) grants residents of the District of Columbia the right to vote in presidential elections.

The **24th Amendment** (1964) prohibits the U.S. government and states from denying citizens the right to vote in federal elections for "failure to pay any poll tax or other tax."

The **25th Amendment** (1967) establishes the order of succession to the presidency if the president or vice president leaves the office. It also provides for the vice president to succeed to the presidency if the president becomes disabled, and it details how presidential disability is determined.

Presidential Succession

The 25th Amendment was put to the test in 1973. Vice President Spiro T. Agnew resigned after pleading no contest to charges of tax fraud. So President Richard M. Nixon appointed Gerald R. Ford, a congressman from Michigan, to replace Agnew. Then, just 10 months later, Nixon resigned because of his role in the Watergate scandal. Vice President Ford became president and appointed Nelson A. Rockefeller, former governor of New York, to the vice presidency.

The **26th Amendment** (1971) grants the right to vote to citizens 18 years of age and older.

The **27th Amendment** (1992) bans midterm congressional pay raises.

The Constitution expands with each amendment, as if it is breathing and growing with the people. This great document has guided the United States through wars, racial strife, bigotry and intolerance, and the unforeseen challenges of a diverse and modern society. Ongoing, unresolved, and new issues continue to shape the Constitution. Proposed amendments to balance the budget, prohibit abortions, permit prayer in public schools, set term limits for members of Congress, prohibit flag burning, and eliminate the Electoral College will live or die according to the wishes of the people.

Supreme Court Justice William J. Brennan Jr. (1956–90) said: "The genius of the Constitution rests not in any static meaning it may have had in a world that is dead and gone, but in the adaptability of its great principles to cope with current problems and present needs."

"Don't interfere with anything in the Constitution. That must be maintained; for it is the only safeguard of our liberties."
—Abraham Lincoln

Branches of Government

The founders of the United States, concerned with the potential abuse of authority, created a representative government that divided the duties among three branches: legislative, executive, and judicial. This *separation of powers* and system of *checks and balances* prevented any one branch from becoming too powerful.

Legislative

The Constitution established a *bicameral* (two-chamber) legislature consisting of the Senate and the House of Representatives so that one chamber might be a check on the other. The Senate has 100 members; two senators are elected from each state. The House of Representatives has 435 members; the number of representatives from each state is based on the population of the state according to the latest census. This plan, which was a result of a compromise at the Constitutional Convention of 1787, ensures that the states are represented in the Senate as coequal members of the Union and in the House as democratically proportional to their populations.

One Person, One Vote

The Constitution does not fix the number of members in the House of Representatives, instead allowing Congress to determine the total. As the population of the United States increased, so did the number of House members. Congress worried that adding more members would cripple the ability to do business in the House, so it passed the Reapportionment Act of 1929 to limit the number to 435 members. Every state is guaranteed at least one representative; the remaining 385 seats are reapportioned (redistributed) among the states after each decennial census (taken every 10 years). Boundaries of congressional districts are redrawn to keep the populations of voting districts equal.

If Congress adjourns its session within 10 days (excluding Sundays) of sending a bill to the president, and the president keeps the bill without signing it, then the bill dies. This is called a *pocket veto.*

Senators are elected to six-year terms. Members of the House are elected to two-year terms. Each term of Congress (numbered consecutively) lasts two years with a new term beginning, according to the 20th Amendment, at noon on the third day of January of every odd-numbered year. Voters elect senators in statewide elections and elect members of the House from their congressional districts.

In addition to the power to pass laws, the Constitution (Article I, Section 8) grants Congress the powers to

- Raise money to run the government.
- Regulate foreign and interstate commerce.
- Determine how aliens become U.S. citizens.
- Provide for and maintain the nation's armed forces.
- Regulate weights and measures.
- Grant copyrights and patents.
- Establish post offices.
- Coin money.
- Declare war.
- Create the lower federal courts.

Executive

The president's chief responsibility is to enforce and administer the laws, but the office carries other responsibilities as well. The Constitution gives the president the *expressed powers* to:

- Serve as commander-in-chief of the nation's armed forces.
- Commission all military officers.
- Appoint the heads of executive departments.
- Appoint ambassadors, Supreme Court justices, and other officials with the consent of the Senate.
- Appoint high-ranking officials to fill vacancies when the Senate is in recess.
- Grant pardons and reprieves for federal crimes.
- Make treaties with the advice and consent of the Senate.
- Inform Congress from time to time about the state of the Union.

How a Bill Becomes a Law

HOUSE

Introduction
H.R. 1 is introduced in the House.

Committee Action
H.R. 1 is referred to a standing committee. It goes to a sub-committee for study, hearings, revisions, and approval. It comes back to the full committee for more hearings and revisions. It then moves to the Rules Committee to set conditions for debate and amendments.

Floor Action
H.R. 1 is debated, then passed or defeated. If passed, H.R. 1 goes to the Senate.

SENATE

Introduction
S. 1 is introduced in the Senate.

Committee Action
S. 1 is referred to a standing committee. It moves to a sub-committee for study, hearings, revisions, and approval. Then it moves back to full committee for more hearings and revisions.

Floor Action
S.1 is debated, then passed or defeated. If passed, S. 1 goes to the House.

Conference Committee
The Conference Committee resolves differences between House and Senate versions of the bill.

Congressional Approval
The House and Senate vote on final passage. The approved bill is sent to the president.

LAW

VETO

X

PRESIDENT

Presidential Action
The president signs, vetoes, or allows the bill to become law without signing it. A vetoed bill returns to Congress. The veto may be overridden by a two-thirds vote of each house.

- Recommend necessary bills.
- Call either or both chambers of Congress into special session, if necessary.
- Act as host to ambassadors and representatives of other nations.

The president also has *implied powers,* including the right to seek opinions of official advisers. The executive departments have developed, by custom and tradition, into an informal advisory body called the Cabinet, with each department headed by a secretary (except the Department of Justice, which is headed by the attorney general). Today, there are 15 executive departments.

The executive branch includes independent agencies, regulatory commissions, and other offices within the Executive Office—including the National Security Council, the Council of Economic Advisors, NASA, and the Office of Management and Budget.

Department	Year Established
State	1789
Treasury	1789
Defense	1789
Justice	1789
Interior	1849
Agriculture	1889
Commerce	1903
Labor	1913
Health and Human Services	1953
Housing and Urban Development	1965
Transportation	1966
Energy	1977
Education	1979
Veterans Affairs	1988
Homeland Security	2002

Judicial

The judicial branch of the U.S. government interprets and applies the laws. Although the Constitution names only the Supreme Court, it authorizes Congress to establish and abolish *inferior*, or lower, federal courts. All of these courts are called *guardians of the Constitution.*

District Courts

The district court is the lowest level of the federal court system. There are 94 courts at this level, and each state (as well as the District of Columbia and Puerto Rico) has at least one district court. Judges appointed by the president preside over these courts and serve for life.

The district courts are the main trial courts in the federal court system. These courts have *original jurisdiction*, or the power to hear a case first—before any other court. The district courts hear criminal and civil cases that involve federal law. These are the only federal courts that regularly use grand juries to indict defendants and petit juries to decide the guilt or innocence of the accused.

A *grand jury* usually consists of 12 to 23 citizens who meet in secret to investigate facts and hear witnesses. This jury determines if the evidence against a person charged with a crime is sufficient to justify a trial. A *petit jury* is a trial jury made up of 12 (sometimes six) citizens. These jurors examine the evidence and make the final decision about the facts in a civil or criminal case.

Courts of Appeals

Congress created the courts of appeals in 1891 to relieve the Supreme Court of the number of cases it heard on appeal directly from the district courts. An *appeal* is a request for the review or rehearing of a case. These courts also review the decisions of federal regulatory agencies such as the Federal Trade Commission.

The 94 district courts are organized into 13 judicial circuits, including the District of Columbia, with one court of appeals (appellate court) for each circuit. Each court of appeals has from six to 28 circuit judges sitting on the court as well as one assigned Supreme Court justice.

Except in connection with their checks on the other branches, the three branches of government have distinct orientations to past, present, and future: The judicial branch is primarily concerned with past actions, the executive branch with present actions, and the legislative branch with future actions.

Supreme Court

The highest level of the federal court system is the Supreme Court. This court is composed of the chief justice of the United States and eight associate justices, all appointed by the president, with the consent of the Senate, to preside for life. Because the justices do not have to worry about being re-elected, they are free to consider the law without the pressures of executive control, public opinion, and political influence.

The Supreme Court hears three kinds of cases:

1. Cases in which the court has *original jurisdiction,* or that involve a representative of another nation or a state as one of the parties
2. Cases appealed from lower federal courts
3. Cases appealed from the highest appeals court in a state

Before 1891, people named these courts the circuit courts of appeals because the Supreme Court justices "rode circuit" (traveled around the judicial district) to hear appeals from the lower courts. Today, the courts of appeals are often still called the circuit courts.

Most federal and state courts in the United States may exercise *judicial review,* which is the important power of deciding the constitutionality of an act of government in any branch. The Supreme Court has the final authority to interpret the meaning of the Constitution and determine if the law is being applied correctly and fairly. For that reason, the Supreme Court is known as "the court of last resort."

Special Courts

Over the years, Congress has created two types of federal courts: constitutional and special courts. Constitutional courts include the courts described above as well as the U.S. Court of International Trade. Special courts—often called legislative courts because Congress created them to help carry out legislative power—hear a narrow range of cases. These courts include the U.S. Court of Appeals for the Armed Forces; the U.S. Court of Appeals for Veterans Claims; the U.S. Court of Federal Claims; the U.S. Tax Court; territorial courts for the Virgin Islands, Guam, and the Northern Marianas; and the courts of the District of Columbia.

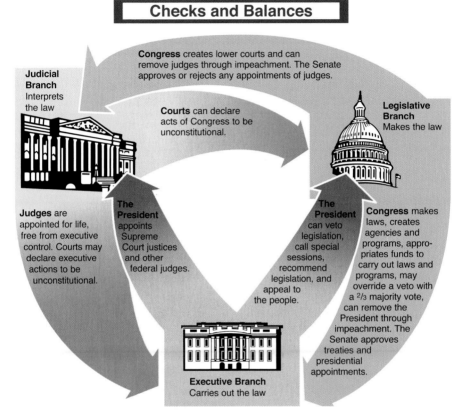

Checks and Balances

Judicial Branch
Interprets the law

Legislative Branch
Makes the law

Executive Branch
Carries out the law

Congress creates lower courts and can remove judges through impeachment. The Senate approves or rejects any appointments of judges.

Courts can declare acts of Congress to be unconstitutional.

Judges are appointed for life, free from executive control. Courts may declare executive actions to be unconstitutional.

The President appoints Supreme Court justices and other federal judges.

The President can veto legislation, call special sessions, recommend legislation, and appeal to the people.

Congress makes laws, creates agencies and programs, appropriates funds to carry out laws and programs, may override a veto with a ⅔ majority vote, can remove the President through impeachment. The Senate approves treaties and presidential appointments.

The People: Partners and Watchdogs

Active citizens provide the most effective check, or restraint, on government actions. The opportunities to get involved with each branch range from support to management and even opposition. Millions of civilians work directly for the government. Others run for public office or campaign for candidates. The best way to participate is to exercise your rights: Vote, serve on juries, attend public hearings, pay attention to what new bills are being considered by Congress, and tell your elected officials how you want them to represent you.

Parties, Splinters, and Special Interests

The framers of the Constitution mistrusted groups of people who united to promote their own narrow causes over the interests of the larger community. James Madison called these groups *factions.* But he knew that trying to abolish the factions would also abolish freedom.

History of American Political Parties

No political parties existed when the Constitution was written, but the people soon split into camps over its ratification. The Federalists, considered the party of the rich and well-born, represented the interests of merchants, bankers, businessmen, and rich plantation owners. They favored a close relationship with Great Britain and a broad interpretation of the Constitution to promote their commercial interests. Federalists believed that property owners should vote, and that ordinary people were too easily influenced to handle much power.

The Anti-Federalists supported the common man—farmers with little acreage and working people in the cities. They thought that if people were educated, they could be trusted to govern themselves. The Anti-Federalists worried that the Federalists, who wanted a strong central government, would destroy republican principles and individual liberties. This made the Anti-Federalists favor a strict interpretation of the Constitution.

By 1796, these two groups became political parties and nominated presidential candidates. The Federalist Party declined in power and disappeared by 1816.

Under Thomas Jefferson's two-term presidential leadership, the Anti-Federalists became known as the Jeffersonian Republicans and remained in power for 40 years. But divisions developed in the party. In the 1820s, supporters of John

"I have already intimated to you the danger of parties in the State. . . ."

—From George Washington's farewell address, 1796

Unlikely Partners

In the presidential election of 1796, the Federalists backed Vice President John Adams for president and the Anti-Federalists backed Thomas Jefferson. Adams beat Jefferson by three electoral votes, so Jefferson became the vice president. Imagine having an elected president and vice president from different parties serving together in the executive branch!

Quincy Adams broke away to form the National Republican Party. When Andrew Jackson ran against Adams, his supporters took the name Democratic-Republicans. After Jackson won, he changed the party name to Democrats. In 1834, the National Republican Party united with other anti-Jackson forces and formed the Whig Party.

The issue of slavery split the Whig Party in the 1850s and fragmented the Democratic Party. Those Whigs who favored slavery left the party and joined pro-slavery Democrats. Those Whigs who opposed it sided with anti-slavery Democrats and created the Republican Party that we recognize today. When Abraham Lincoln was elected in 1860 as the first Republican president, he ended the long era of Democratic control.

The Democratic Party survived in the South but was crippled by the Civil War. The party slowly built up its base of voters while the Republicans dominated national politics for almost 75 years.

The 1932 election marked a big change in the public's attitude about the role of government. During the Great Depression, which began in 1929, the unemployment rate was high—33 percent. People wanted the government to help them find jobs and take care of their families. When Franklin Delano Roosevelt's victory brought the Democrats back to power, his New Deal programs put Americans to work and expanded the social and economic responsibilities of the national government. For the next 36 years, Republicans criticized the Democrats from the sidelines for their "big government" and "bureaucracy."

Since the late 1960s, control of the national government has been divided. If one party had the White House, the other party held the majority of seats in Congress. Although the Founding Fathers did not foresee the rise of political parties, they created a government that separated the powers of political parties and a system of checks and balances.

Two-Party System

The American political system started as a two-party system, and the current election process follows this structure. People form political parties to control government by winning elections and holding public offices. If one party gets control of the executive and legislative branches, it can direct public policy and enact laws to advance the party's position. If different parties have control of Congress and the Executive Office, the elected officials must compromise to get anything accomplished. A two-party system, rather than a government splintered by multiple parties, makes compromise much easier.

In most elections, voters can choose only one candidate for an office, and only one candidate can win that office. Many people think voting for a third-party candidate who has little chance of winning is wasting their vote. Also, Republicans and Democrats are able to work together to enact election laws that make it more difficult for third-party candidates to get their names on the ballots. In fact, non-major party candidates have appeared on the ballot in every state only seven times in the history of American presidential elections. While it's more difficult for these minor party candidates to get on the ballot, they are still a part of the system and many have large followings.

Minor Parties

A *minor party* is a cross between a major political party and a special-interest group. It generally forms around an ideology or an issue, and then becomes a party to nominate its own candidates for public office. Minor parties are:

- Ideological, such as the Libertarian Party

- Single-issue, such as the Right to Life Party

- Economic protest, such as the Populist Party

- Splinter, such as the Progressive Party

The Political Party Family Tree

Today's Democrats and Republicans have their roots in opposite party philosophies. Although the Democrats are direct descendants of Thomas Jefferson's republican philosophies, they also borrow Federalist ideas about a strong federal government and broad interpretation of the Constitution. Present-day Republicans have taken Jefferson's views supporting "less government" as their own platform.

"No party can fool all of the people all of the time. That's why we have two parties."

—Bob Hope (1903–2003), comedian who entertained 12 presidents during his lifetime

When the Republican Party nominated *incumbent* (current) President William Howard Taft as its candidate for the 1912 election, former President Theodore Roosevelt broke away from the Republican Party to run for president on his own

A strong third-party candidate can have a great impact on an election. In 2000, Ralph Nader ran for president as the Green Party candidate against Republican George W. Bush and Democrat Al Gore. Nader received 3 percent of the popular vote but received no electoral votes. Gore won the popular vote, but Bush collected the most Electoral College votes and became president. Having a third-party candidate made this an extraordinarily close election.

"Bull Moose" Progressive Party ballot. Roosevelt's move split the Republican vote, allowing Woodrow Wilson, a Democrat, to win the presidency.

Unlike the two major political parties, minor parties are willing to take a stand on controversial issues. They draw the public's attention to problems that the major parties might try to avoid. As often happens, the two major parties steal the positions of minor parties on those issues that stir the public's interest.

Minor parties serve important functions in the political system, but the Republican Party is the only party in American political history to rise from being a third party to becoming a major political party.

Special-Interest Groups

People who share an interest often band together. *Special-interest groups* form around a cause or an issue to help shape public policy. These groups try to persuade elected officials to respond to their particular concerns and to pass legislation that will promote their causes.

Unlike political parties, special-interest groups do not nominate candidates for public office. They are private organizations—only accountable to their members—that focus on issues, not people. In fact, they are concerned with only those issues and policies that directly affect the interests of the group members. The groups may, however, support candidates who support their positions.

These groups are as varied as their interests. Some examples are:

- Business groups: Chamber of Commerce, National Association of Manufacturers
- Trade associations: National Restaurant Association, American Trucking Associations
- Labor organizations: Fraternal Order of Police, American Federation of Labor–Congress of Industrial Organizations (AFL–CIO)
- Agricultural groups: American Farm Bureau Federation, National Grange
- Professional associations: American Medical Association, American Bar Association
- Religious organizations: National Council of Churches, American Jewish Congress

Some special-interest groups promote the welfare of specific groups (American Association of Retired Persons); promote or oppose certain causes (Sierra Club or The Brady Center to Prevent Gun Violence; and advance public-interest issues (Common Cause).

Special-interest groups raise awareness about public policies that promote or threaten their causes. They serve as another facet of the checks and balances system by keeping tabs on public agencies and officials. These groups are another effective way for citizens to participate in politics.

As James Madison knew when he drafted the First Amendment (guaranteeing the rights to assemble and to petition the government), special-interest "factions" compete with one another in the public arena and actually counterbalance and moderate extreme points of view.

Campaigning on Infomercials

Ross Perot ran for president and started his own movement, the Reform Party, in 1992. He frequently appeared on television with flash cards to educate the public about the national budget deficit and explain his own economic plan to balance the federal budget. Perot captured nearly 20 percent of the vote. Although Perot did not win, he tapped into public dissatisfaction with elected officials and put the issue of fiscal (financial) responsibility on the public agenda.

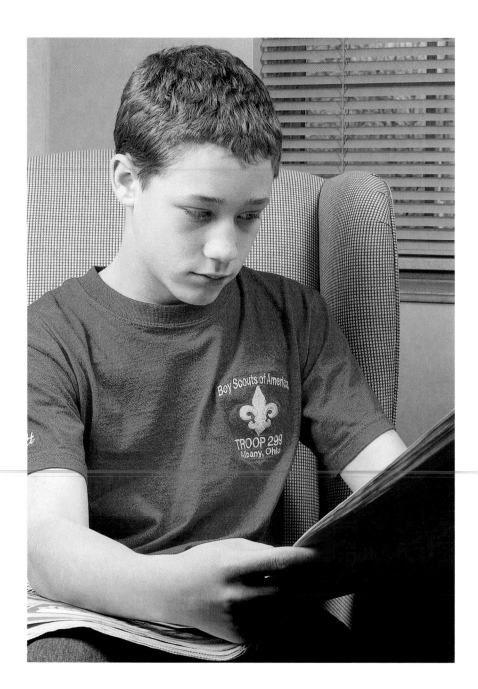

National Issues

As you watch the evening news on television or read a news-paper, consider how the national issues covered relate to what you have already read in this merit badge pamphlet. Do the topics affect a citizen's rights and freedoms? Have new bills been proposed in Congress? Are the senators and the president deadlocked over an issue like health care or Social Security? Did the Supreme Court rule on a controversial case? Which Cabinet department dominates the news?

In countries where freedom of the press and the right to free speech do not exist, the government controls mass media. Citizens know only what their leaders are willing to tell them. But in the United States, citizens have the right to know the truth.

> If you want your opinion and your vote to matter, you must make consistent efforts to seek informa-tion. If you want to keep your rights and freedoms, you must act.

Mass Media

The vast communication network that reaches large audiences of diverse individuals at the same time through television, newspapers, radio, magazines, and the internet is called *mass media.* These communication channels provide much entertainment, but they are also important sources of political information.

Although they don't exist to influence the government, the mass media have the power to focus the public's attention on certain issues. By telling audiences not what to think, but what to think *about,* the media help to shape the *public agenda.*

The public agenda is the list of those issues that elected officials and citizens agree need governmental attention.

Even though requirement 3 asks you to track the evening news on television OR read a daily newspaper, try to compare on one day how a specific national issue is covered on television and in the newspaper. You will probably discover that television touches lightly on the topic and presents brief bits of information. In a newspaper, reporters—like their readers—have more opportunity to explore the issue in detail.

Fact or Opinion?

Learn how to recognize *propaganda* so that you do not accept biased information as fact. Political parties and special-interest groups want to persuade you to agree with them. Read newspaper editorials to figure out what issues and candidates the paper supports. Think about whether the news report presents a one-sided or balanced view. Are conclusions supported by concrete information, or are opinions based on selected facts?

Speeches of National Historical Importance

Great leaders, great orators, and great speechwriters can mark the importance of a historical moment so that it is fixed in our memories. Certain speeches express the conscience and spirit of a people. Others warn about oppression (domination), memorialize fallen soldiers, or uplift a discouraged nation. These speeches urge citizens to take action, inspire, and redirect history.

Throughout this merit badge pamphlet, you have read quotes from famous speeches. Consider reading those speeches in their entirety. Or choose another speech such as:

- Martin Luther King Jr.'s "I Have a Dream" speech in which he calls for an end to segregation and racial discrimination

- Franklin Delano Roosevelt's speech one day after the bombing of Pearl Harbor, asking Congress to declare war on Japan

- Ronald Reagan's "Tear Down This Wall" speech that challenged Communist leaders to end the Cold War and foster peace between West and East Germany

Voicing Your Own Opinion

It is our privilege as American citizens to contact our elected representatives and expect an answer. You can find out how to contact your senators or the representative from your congressional district by looking in the government (blue) pages of your local telephone book or on the internet (with your parent's permission).

Choose a national issue that interests you and gather the facts before contacting your public official. Try to learn as much as you can about all sides of the issue before forming an opinion. The Web sites for the U.S. Senate and the U.S. House of Representatives make it simple to contact your representatives by e-mail. You can write a letter online or send a letter by mail.

To write an effective letter, follow these tips.

- Address the official using his or her correct title.

    U.S. Senator

    The address: The Honorable John Smith

    The greeting: Dear Senator Smith:

    Member of the House of Representatives

    The address: The Honorable Mary Doe

    The greeting: Dear Ms. Doe:

- Identify yourself and your reasons for writing the letter.

- Refer to a specific bill by number or name, if applicable.

- Explain—briefly, rationally, politely—why you are concerned about the issue.

- Send your letter before the bill is brought to the floor or while your representative can still do something about your concern.

- Request a response and include your return address.

    Senators and representatives want to know what you think, but they receive thousands of letters each month. An aide probably will answer your letter. However, you may have an opportunity to contact your congressional representative in person if he or she is visiting the local field office.

National Treasures and Other Government Structures

An important way for U.S. citizens to appreciate their hard-won rights and freedoms is to visit the sites where major historical events took place and where people from different cultures settled, or tour public buildings and observe firsthand their government officials at work.

Although books, photographs, and virtual tours on the internet help us understand our heritage, nothing compares to the experience of standing on a Civil War battlefield, touring the White House, or exploring the Anasazi cliff dwellings built in the Southwest more than a thousand years ago.

Your family may have lived in this country for hundreds of years or for 20 years. It does not matter. If you are a U.S. citizen, you share a heritage with every other American citizen. So go see some of the significant public buildings, historical parks, landmarks, and monuments. After all, these national treasures are our connections with this country's past.

Landmarks and Monuments

The National Park Service, which is part of the U.S. Department of the Interior, is in charge of national parks as well as certain historic settings. Besides protecting those scenic parks valued for their spectacular natural features, such as Yellowstone National Park, the National Park Service identifies and preserves all the historic buildings and sites that have national importance—that is, those places that mean something to most Americans. The National Park Service maintains an official list of cultural resources worth preserving called the National Register of Historic Places. Three percent of the properties listed are designated as National Historic Landmarks.

What's the Difference?

National Historic Landmark—a particular site, structure, or object of national importance (Vietnam Veterans Memorial)

National Monument—an area preserved for its historic, prehistoric, or scientific interest that includes at least one resource of national importance (Fort Sumter National Monument)

National Historic Site—a place of national historical significance, usually with a single primary feature (Ford's Theatre)

National Historical Park—a larger, more complex area than a National Historic Site, it includes several areas and features of national historical importance (Independence National Historical Park in Philadelphia)

Before you head for one of the National Historic Landmarks or National Monuments, call to find out if visitors are allowed. Schedules for tours vary and are always subject to change.

Government Facilities

Public buildings include a variety of government facilities such as the Johnson Space Center, Federal Reserve banks, the Library of Congress, and federal courthouses. Even if you live in a small town, you probably can find a federal facility, such as a post office, that serves the local community.

When you visit a federal facility, you see your government working for you. Think about how the activity in that building or on that site affects your life.

Preservation

American citizens have a debt to the people who came before us, and an obligation to the generations to follow. National landmarks and monuments are places to experience history. Many are endangered, but they deserve to be preserved for what they represent as part of America's history and culture. You can help preserve these places by joining a local or national historic preservation organization and by volunteering to work at one of the historic landmarks.

Preserving national sites is only a part of preserving America's heritage. As a good citizen, you must guard your rights and celebrate your freedom. Stand up for others. Seek information. Become a concerned citizen.

The American people made their own government. It is still a work in progress, but it bends and embraces its citizens. You have the right, the duty, and the privilege to help shape your government. Value your freedom.

As Thomas Paine wrote in his *Common Sense* pamphlets of 1776: "The cause of America is in a great measure the cause of all mankind. . . .We have it in our power to begin the world again."

Mount Rushmore

Resources

Scouting Literature

The Constitution of the United States;
American Business, American Cultures,
American Heritage, Citizenship in the
Community, Citizenship in the World,
and *Law* merit badge pamphlets

For more information about
Scouting-related resources, visit
the BSA's online retail catalog
(with your parent's permission)
at http://www.scoutstuff.org.

Books

Feinberg, Barbara Silberdick. *The Articles of Confederation: The First Constitution of the United States.* Twenty-First Century Books, 2002.

Freedman, Russell. *Give Me Liberty! The Story of the Declaration of Independence.* Holiday House, 2000.

Jaffe, Steven H. *Who Were the Founding Fathers? Two Hundred Years of Reinventing American History.* Henry Holt and Co., 1996.

Kassinger, Ruth. *U.S. Census: A Mirror of America.* Raintree Steck-Vaughn Publishers, 2000.

Krull, Kathleen. *A Kid's Guide to America's Bill of Rights: Curfews, Censorship, and the 100-Pound Giant.* William Morrow & Co., 1999.

Mackintosh, Barry. *The National Park Service.* Chelsea House Publishers, 1988.

Maestro, Betty. *A More Perfect Union: The Story of Our Constitution.* HarperCollins, 2008.

McHugh, Erin. *National Parks: A Kid's Guide to America's Parks, Monuments and Landmarks.* Black Dog & Leventhal, 2012.

McIntire, Suzanne, ed. *The American Heritage Book of Great American Speeches for Young People.* Jossey-Bass, 2001.

Panchyk, Richard. *Keys to American History: Understanding Our Most Important Historic Documents.* Chicago Review Press, 2009.

Selzer, Adam. *The Smart Aleck's Guide to American History.* Delacorte Books for Young Readers, 2009.

Zeinert, Karen. *Free Speech: From Newspapers to Music Lyrics.* Enslow Publishers, 1995.

Organizations and Websites

American Civil Liberties Union
125 Broad St., 18th Floor
New York, NY 10004
Telephone: 212-549-2500
Website: http://www.aclu.org

Congress.gov
Website: http://www.congress.gov

Democratic National Committee
Telephone: 202-863-8000
Website: http://www.democrats.org

GovSpot
Website: http://www.govspot.com

League of Women Voters
Telephone: 202-429-1965
Website: http://www.lwv.org

National Constitution Center
525 Arch St.
Independence Mall
Philadelphia, PA 19106
Telephone: 215-409-6600
Website:
http://www.constitutioncenter.org

National Park Service
1849 C St. NW
Washington, DC 20240
Telephone: 202-208-6843
Website: http://www.nps.gov

Republican National Committee
Telephone: 202-863-8500
Website: http://www.rnc.org

U.S. Census Bureau
4600 Silver Hill Road
Washington, DC 20233-4600
Telephone: 301-763-4636
Website: http://www.census.gov

The U.S. Constitution Online
Website: http://www.usconstitution.net

U.S. House of Representatives
Telephone: 202-224-3121
Website: http://www.house.gov

U.S. Government Printing Office
Telephone: 202-512-0018
Website: http://www.gpoaccess.gov

U.S. Senate
Telephone: 202-224-3121
Website: http://www.senate.gov

U.S. Supreme Court
Telephone: 202-479-3000
Website: http://www.supremecourt.gov

USA.gov
Website: http://www.usa.gov

The White House
1600 Pennsylvania Ave. NW
Washington, DC 20500
Telephone: 202-456-1414
Website: http://www.whitehouse.gov

Acknowledgments

For this new edition of the *Citizenship in the Nation* merit badge pamphlet, the Boy Scouts of America thanks Harry C. Boyte, Center for Democracy and Citizenship, Humphrey Institute, for sharing his time, expertise, and assistance.

The Boy Scouts of America is grateful to the men and women serving on the Merit Badge Maintenance Task Force for the improvements made in updating this pamphlet.

Photo and Illustration Credits

Shutterstock.com, courtesy—cover (*vote button*, ©Augusto Cabral; *flag*, ©jejim; *scale*, ©Olivier Le Queinec; *Statue of Liberty*, ©Tutti Frutti); cover and page 23 (*U.S. Capitol*, ©Kim Seidl); pages 4 (*Statue of Liberty and flag*, ©Delpixel), 6 (©Zoran Karapancev), 41 (©James Steidl), and 45 (*Mount Rushmore*, ©Francesco Dazzi)

All other photos not mentioned above are the property of the Boy Scouts of America.

John McDearmon—page 27

Randy Piland—pages 8, 9, 10, 24 (*Scout with sculpture*), 33, 38, 42, 45 (*Scout at Cutler Hall*), and 48